BRASS

AN INTRODUCTION TO MUSICAL INSTRUMENTS

By Dee Lillegard

2166

CP CHILDRENS PRESS ®

CHICAGO

PHOTO CREDITS

Library of Congress Cataloging-in-Publication Data

Lillegard, Dee.
   Brass / by Dee Lillegard.
        p.   cm. — (An introduction to musical
instruments)
   Summary: A brief introduction to each of the brass
instruments.
   ISBN 0-516-02218-0
   1. Brass instruments—Juvenile
literature. [1. Brass
instruments.] I. Title. II. Series: Lillegard, Dee.
Introduction to musical instruments.
ML933.L54   1988   87-32990
788'.01—dc19   CIP
                                    AC MN

Squeeze your lips together.
Now blow through them. Let
your breath come through
like the wind.

That is what you must do
to play **brass instruments.**

*As you learn to play a brass instrument, you will
learn to breathe correctly, too.*

Brass instruments are wind
instruments. They are made of
a metal called brass.

You blow through mouthpieces
shaped like cups.

Place your lips on the
mouthpiece in a special way.
You tighten or loosen your lips
to make different notes.

Bugles are brass instruments.

Your tongue is used to start
and stop the notes.

Your fingers are important, too. Most **brass instruments** have valves. You push them up and down with your fingers. The valves make more notes than you can make with your lips alone.

You can change the tone of
a **brass instrument** with a *mute*.
Put a mute into the bell of
the instrument. Its sound will
soften.

Let's look at the **brass
instruments**. The **trumpet** is
the loudest of the brasses.
It also plays the highest notes.

Its sound can be bold and bright. But it can be soft and smooth, too. You need strong lips to play the **trumpet**.

Trumpets date back to about 1200 B.C..

The cornet is played in military and concert bands.

The **cornet** looks like a
trumpet. But it is shorter.
Its sound is softer and more
mellow. If you can play a
trumpet, you can play a **cornet**.

The **trombone** is different.
It has no valves. It has a
slide that is pulled in and
out.

The **trombone** makes a
lower sound than a **trumpet**.
Its deep sounds can be played
loudly or softly. You need
strong lips and long arms
to play a **trombone**!

15

The **baritone horn** makes
a sound like the **trombone**.
But it doesn't have a slide.
It can be played faster
than a **trombone** because it
has valves, like a **trumpet**.

The slide makes the
trombone longer. Horns are
really tubes. Longer tubes
make deeper sounds. Valves
add more notes to **brass
instruments**.

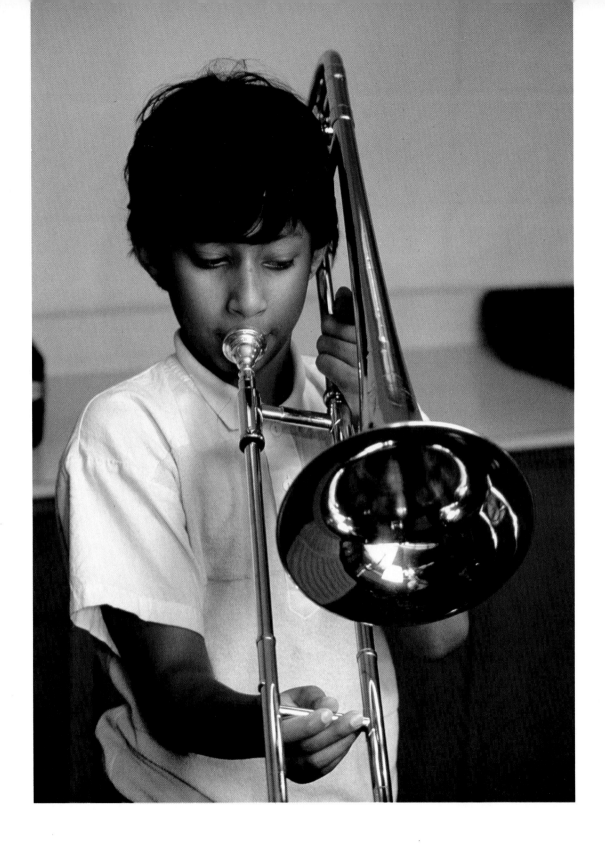

If we could straighten out
a **French horn**, it would be
twelve feet long. Twisting
and folding the long tube
makes it easier to handle.

Sometimes the **French horn** is just called "the horn." It makes a soft sound. Put your hand inside the bell to muffle, or mute, the sound.

It's hard to play the
French horn. But it sounds
beautiful in a symphony
orchestra or a small group.

Hear the deep, foghorn
sound? It's the **tuba**.

The **tuba** is the lowest of
the **brass instruments**. It is
a sixteen-feet-long tube with
a big bell. The **tuba** is not so
hard to play. But it's heavy.

If you can play the **tuba**,
you can play the **sousaphone**.
The **sousaphone** is the **tuba's**
big brother. It curls around
your head and rests on your
shoulder. It's easier to
carry in a parade.

The **bugle** is a **trumpet** without valves. It can play only the "lip notes." **Bugles** have been used to wake up soldiers—or scouts at camp.

Play the **trumpet** and
wake somebody up!
Use your lips, your
tongue, your breath, your
fingers. Use them all

together to make music. Play
in a small band, a marching
band, or a symphony orchestra.
The shining **brass instruments**
can be fun!

🎼 WIND INSTRUMENTS

🎼 PERCUSSION INSTRUMENTS

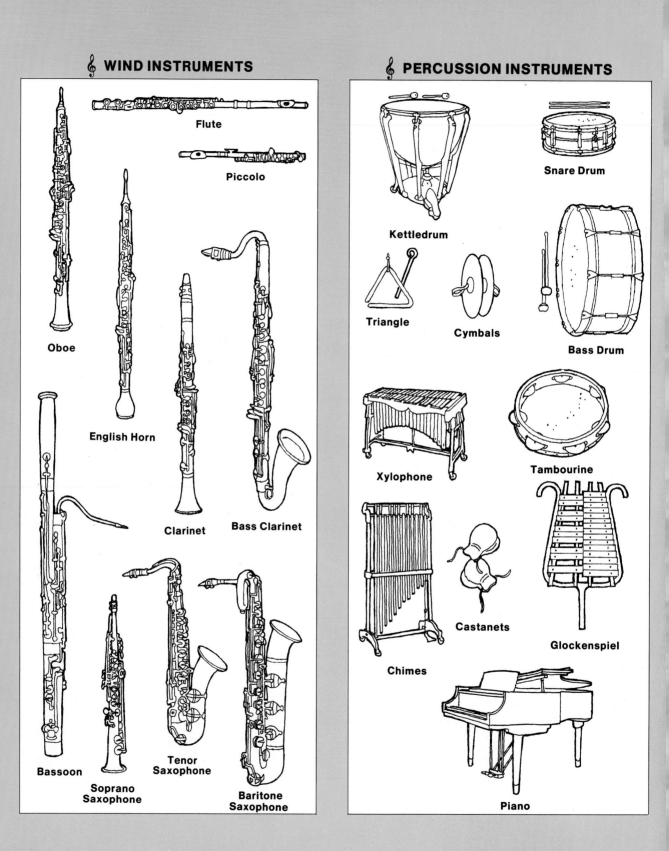

Flute

Piccolo

Oboe

English Horn

Clarinet

Bass Clarinet

Bassoon

Soprano Saxophone

Tenor Saxophone

Baritone Saxophone

Kettledrum

Snare Drum

Triangle

Cymbals

Bass Drum

Xylophone

Tambourine

Chimes

Castanets

Glockenspiel

Piano

♪ STRINGED INSTRUMENTS

♪ BRASS INSTRUMENTS

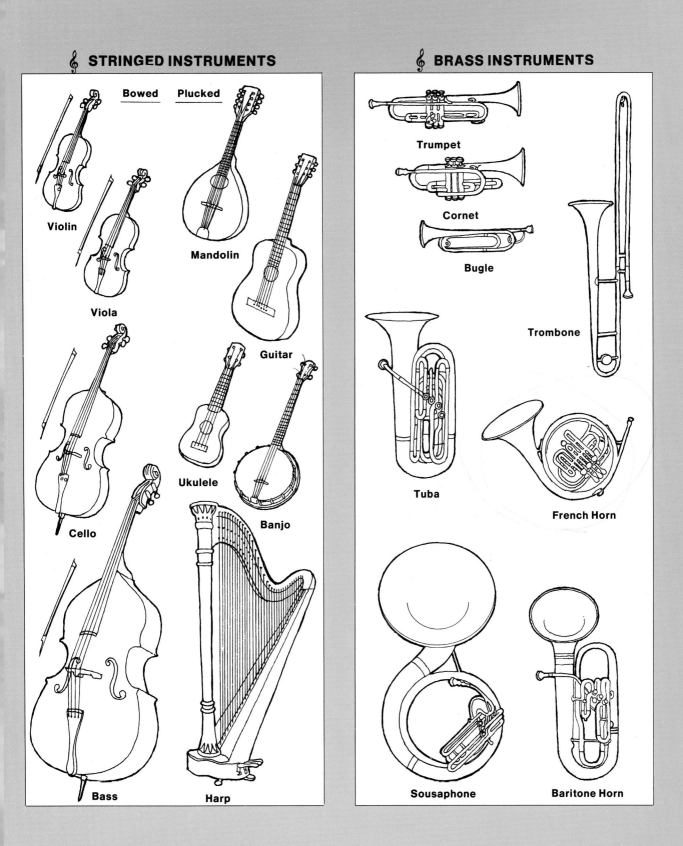

Bowed   Plucked

Violin

Viola

Mandolin

Guitar

Cello

Ukulele

Banjo

Bass

Harp

Trumpet

Cornet

Bugle

Trombone

Tuba

French Horn

Sousaphone

Baritone Horn

ABOUT THE AUTHOR

Dee Lillegard (born Deanna Quintel) is the author of over two hundred published stories, poems, and puzzles for children, plus *Word Skills*, a series of high-interest grammar worktests, and *September to September*, *Poems for All Year Round*, a teacher resource. Ms. Lillegard has also worked as a children's book editor and teaches writing for children in the San Francisco Bay area. She is a native Californian.